KU-524-739

Hot & Spicy

POCKET COOKERY GUIDE

Hot & Spicy

MARSHALL CAVENDISH

This edition produced by
Marshall Cavendish Books
(a division of
Marshall Cavendish
Partworks Ltd).

First printed 1996

ISBN 1-85435-871-5

British Library Cataloguing
in Publication Data:
A catalogue record for this
book is available from the
British Library

Printed and bound in Singapore

Some of this material has
previously appeared in the
Marshall Cavendish partwork
The Two in One
Cookery Collection

Contents

Foreword

Spices are fundamental to the dishes that are described in the following pages. By using them in different combinations, each of the recipes is embued with a distinctive flavour. Spices can be used to enliven the flavours of grains and pulses, or to enhance most vegetables, fish, or meat. The range of tastes the spices offer is almost infinite – according to your preferences, you can use them to produce a dish that is deliciously aromatic, or one to set your taste buds on fire.

Dozens of spices are now available, from specialist shops and even from supermarkets. You can use the commercially ground ones if you wish, but it is simple enough to buy whole spices and grind them yourself just before cooking - their flavour and aroma will be far more intense.

A small coffee grinder will grind spices in a few seconds; grinding by hand with the traditional pestle and mortar takes a bit longer. Store spices in a cool, dry place and use them quickly while they are still aromatic.

The Food of Mexico

Mexican food is as complex and exciting as the country itself. Early settlers grew sweetcorn, peppers, squashes, avocados and potatoes. They also grew tomatoes and beans, now essential ingredients in many recipes.

Chilli peppers are native to Central America, and Mexican cooking would not be the same without them. They grow in many shapes and sizes; most are hot and can produce anything from a warm glow to a burning sensation. French, Spanish, Aztec and Mayan cuisine has also had an influence on many Mexican recipes.

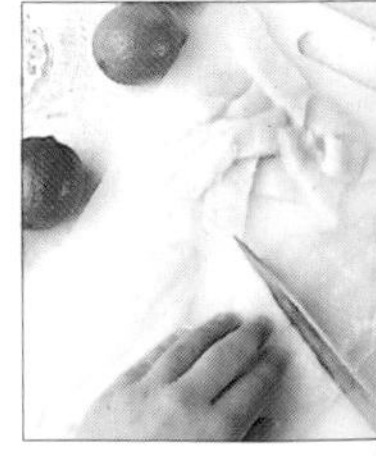

Tortillas are the bread of Mexico. Made with corn or wheat, they look like thin pancakes, and accompany most meals. When cooked and stuffed they become complete and tasty dishes.

Contents

Chunky Gazpacho

IDEAL FOR SLIMMERS OR FOR HEALTHY SUMMER EATING, GAZPACHO IS LOW IN FAT AND HIGH IN VITAMIN C

SERVES 4

35 MINS TO PREPARE, PLUS CHILLING

195 KCAL PER SERVING

SUITABLE FOR VEGETARIANS

8 large salad tomatoes
boiling water
2 garlic cloves, chopped
1 green pepper, de-seeded and chopped
1 cucumber, peeled, seeded and chopped
1 tbls chopped fresh parsley
1 tbls chopped fresh mint
50g / 2oz fresh white breadcrumbs
2 tbls wine vinegar
2 tbls olive oil
275ml / ½pt iced water
salt and freshly ground white pepper
ice cubes, optional

for the garnish:
2 hard-boiled eggs
1 onion
12 black olives
1 red pepper

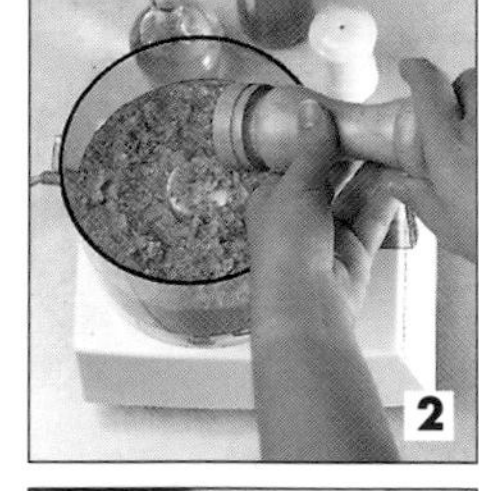

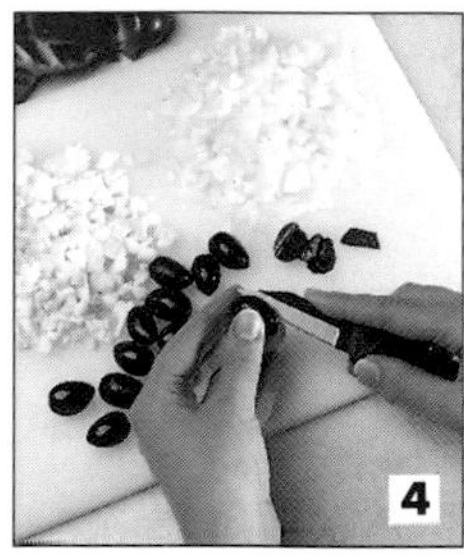

1 Put the tomatoes in a bowl and cover with boiling water. Leave for 2 minutes. Remove and, if the skins have not split, pierce with a fork or skewer. Peel away the skins before the tomatoes get too cold, cut into quarters and de-seed.

2 Put all the ingredients, except the iced water, salt and pepper and ice cubes, into a blender or food processor, in two batches if necessary, and blend at low speed for 30 - 60 seconds or until smooth.

3 Turn the mixture into a large serving bowl and add the iced water, season to taste, cover and chill for at least 2 hours.

4 To prepare the garnishes, chop the eggs, finely dice the onion, stone and chop the olives and finely dice the red pepper. Just before serving, add a few ice cubes to the soup if you wish and serve, accompanied by the garnishes.

SERVING SUGGESTIONS

The garnishes served with Chunky Gazpacho are stirred into the soup as it is about to be eaten. Put them in separate bowls on the table so that each diner can pick the garnishes of their choice.

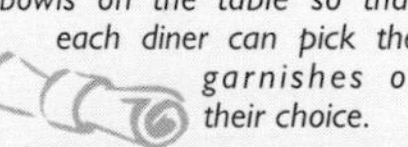

COOK'S TIPS

Traditionally, this soup was prepared by hand, using a mortar and pestle. The advent of the electric blender has changed all that and now Gazpacho is quick to make. If you use a mortar and pestle, pound the ingredients in the order listed, adding the vinegar and oil drop by drop. When the ingredients are thoroughly blended, stir in the iced water and chill.

Traditional Guacamole

THIS CREAMY YET SPICY AVOCADO SALAD MAKES A GREAT DIP TO SERVE WITH TORTILLA CHIPS, CRISPS OR CRUDITÉS

SERVES
4

20 MINS
TO PREPARE

200 KCAL
PER
SERVING

SUITABLE
FOR
VEGETARIANS

1 beef tomato or 2 large tomatoes
boiling water
4 spring onions
1 green chilli
1 garlic clove
3 small or 2 large avocados
1 tbls lemon or lime juice
1 tbls chopped fresh coriander, plus extra to garnish
1 tsp paprika
salt and pepper

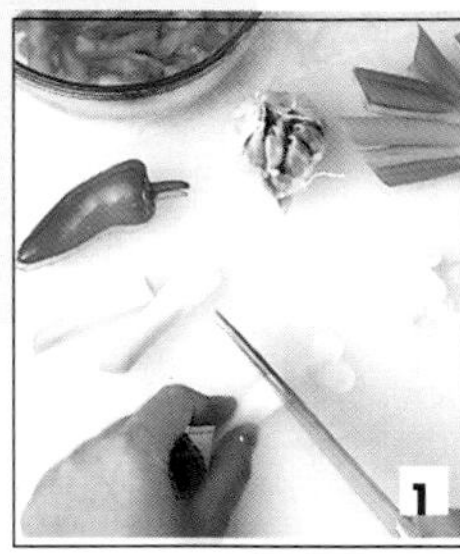

1 Put the tomato in a bowl and cover with the boiling water. Leave for 2 minutes. Remove and, if the skins have not split, pierce with a fork or skewer. Peel away the skins, cut into quarters and de-seed, then chop. Cut off the green parts of the spring onion and discard. Finely slice the white parts. Using rubber gloves, de-seed and finely chop the chilli. Finely chop the garlic.

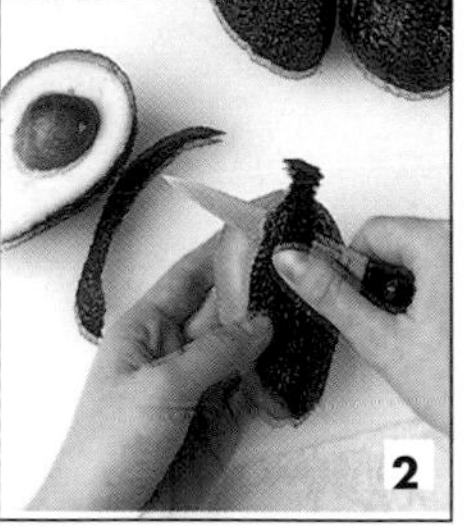

2 Halve and peel the avocados, then remove the stones. Roughly chop the flesh and place in a blender or food processor, then immediately add the lemon or lime juice, tomato, spring onion, chilli, garlic, coriander and paprika.

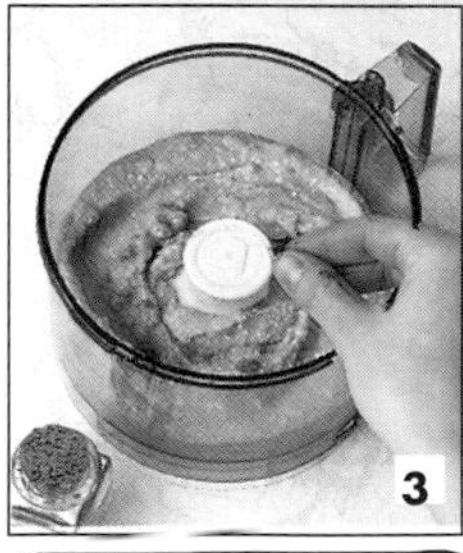

3 Process quickly until the ingredients are well mixed but not completely smooth. Season with salt and pepper to taste and serve at once.

COOK'S TIPS

The citrus juice is an important part of this recipe — it's added immediately after the avocados because it helps prevent them turning brown. Gucacamole is best made immediately before serving but, if you are making it in advance, you can slow down discoloration by leaving one of the avocado stones in the dip – just don't forget to remove the stone before serving! Another tip is to drizzle a tablespoonful of olive oil over the Guacamole, covering the surface.

WHAT TO DRINK

This Mexican dip is best served with a light red wine such as Beaujolais, or a chilled Mexican lager such as Dos Equis.

Three-bean Salad

THIS TASTY AND COLOURFUL SALAD OF BLACK BEANS, RED KIDNEY BEANS AND CHICKPEAS IS ENLIVENED BY A FRESH, TANGY DRESSING

SERVES 4 - 6

25 MINS TO PREPARE, PLUS SOAKING

1 - 3 HRS TO COOK

360 KCAL PER SERVING

SUITABLE FOR VEGETARIANS

100g / 4oz dried black beans
100g / 4oz dried red kidney beans
100g / 4oz dried chickpeas
1 yellow pepper, seeded
2 tbls chopped parsley
6 spring onions, chopped
3 celery sticks, chopped

for the dressing:
3 tbls olive oil
1 tbls lemon juice
1 tsp wholegrain mustard
½ tsp honey salt and pepper

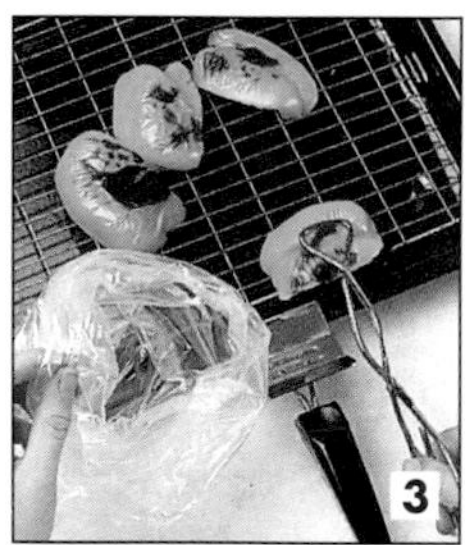

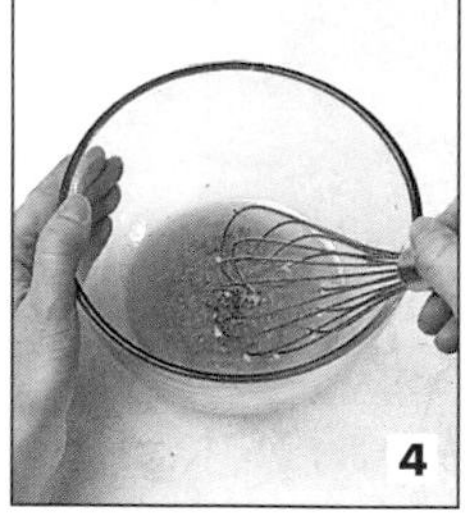

1 Keeping the beans separate, wash well, place in bowls and cover with plenty of cold water. Leave to soak for at least 8 hours or overnight.

2 Drain the beans and rinse well. Cook the beans separately, placing each in a large saucepan and covering with about 1.7L/3pt water. Bring to the boil and cook rapidly for 10–15 minutes. Reduce the heat, partially cover the pans and simmer until tender. The black beans will take about 1 hour to cook and the kidney beans around 1½ hours, while the chickpeas could take anywhere from 1 to 3 hours, possibly more if they are old. As soon as each type is cooked, drain well.

3 Meanwhile, cut the pepper into quarters lengthwise. Grill under high heat until the skin is blistered and blackened. Put the pepper quarters in a polythene bag, seal and leave to cool, then peel away the skin and slice the pepper. Mix the beans and pepper strips together in a bowl.

4 Whisk together the oil, lemon juice, mustard, honey and salt and pepper to taste and pour over the warm beans. Leave to cool.

5 Add the parsley, spring onions and celery to the beans and toss together gently. Adjust the seasoning and serve.

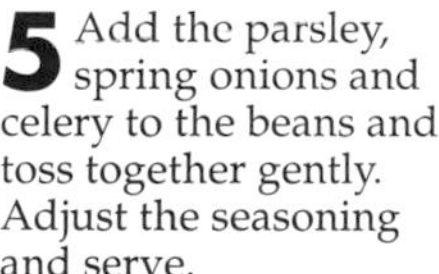

VARIATIONS

If time is short, ready-cooked canned beans may be used instead of dried. Use 400g/14oz tins of chickpeas, red kidney beans and flageolet beans (ready cooked black beans are not easy to find).

If you warm the beans in their canning liquid, then drain before adding the dressing, you'll find that they absorb the flavours better.

COOK'S TIPS

Dried beans – particularly red and black kidney beans – should be boiled rapidly for 10–15 minutes, then simmered until tender. The fast boiling will destroy toxic substances contained in the skins and make them perfectly safe to eat.

Spicy Bean Burritos

TASTY TORTILLAS ARE FILLED WITH SPICY BEANS, GRATED CHEESE, SOUR CREAM AND SALAD TO MAKE THIS TRADITIONAL MEXICAN DISH

SERVES 4

1 HR TO PREPARE

45 MINS TO COOK

860 KCAL PER SERVING

for the tortillas:
225g / ½lb flour, plus extra for dusting
1 tsp salt
40g / 1½oz lard, diced
125ml / 4fl oz warm water

for the filling:
2 tbls vegetable oil
1 large onion, chopped
2 garlic cloves, crushed
2 x 430g / 15½oz tins red kidney beans in chilli sauce
100g /4oz Cheddar cheese, coarsely grated
150ml / 5fl oz sour cream
½ iceberg lettuce, shredded
4 tomatoes, chopped
4 spring onions, chopped

3

4

1 Sift the flour and salt into a large bowl and rub in the lard with your fingertips until the mixture resembles fine breadcrumbs. Stir in the water, 1 tbls at a time, and use your fingertips to make a soft dough. Divide into 8 equal pieces and knead each one on a lightly floured work surface for 5 minutes or until smooth and pliable. Roll each into a smooth ball and place on a plate.

2 Heat the oil in a saucepan over medium heat and fry the onion and garlic for 10 minutes or until golden, stirring often. Add the beans and heat through, stirring occasionally. Mash with a potato masher or fork and keep warm.

3 Working with one ball at a time, roll out the tortilla dough into 25cm/10in rounds, dusting occasionally with flour to prevent sticking. As each one is shaped, stack on a plate with a piece of greaseproof paper between each one, making sure you cover the top one.

4 Bring a saucepan of water to the boil, lower the heat to a simmer and place a heatproof plate on top. Heat a 25cm/10in non-stick frying pan over medium heat until a drop of water sizzles when it is sprinkled in the pan. Put the tortillas, one at a time, into the pan and cook for 2 minutes or until bubbles appear on the surface. Using a spatula, turn over and continue cooking for 2 minutes or until the tortilla slides around the pan and is flecked with brown. Transfer the tortilla to the plate over the pan to keep warm and cover with greaseproof paper. Continue in this way until all the tortillas are cooked and stacked on the plate, with a sheet of greaseproof paper between each.

5 To assemble the burritos, lay a tortilla on your work surface and place 3 tbls bean mixture in the centre. Top with 2 tbls cheese, 1 tbls soured cream and some lettuce, tomato and spring onion. Fold opposite sides of the tortilla to meet in the centre, then fold one end under. Transfer to a warm serving dish. Continue until all the tortillas are filled. Serve warm.

Lime Sole Seviche

FRESH LIME JUICE IS USED TO 'COOK' LEMON SOLE FILLETS IN THIS SIMPLE, TRADITIONAL MEXICAN FISH DISH

SERVES
4

25 MINS
TO PREPARE,
PLUS MARINATING

225 KCAL
PER
SERVING

450g / 1 lb lemon sole fillets
4 limes
1 large tomato
boiling water
1 red chilli, seeded and chopped
1 onion
4 tbls olive oil
1 tbls white wine vinegar
2 tbls chopped fresh coriander, plus a sprig to garnish

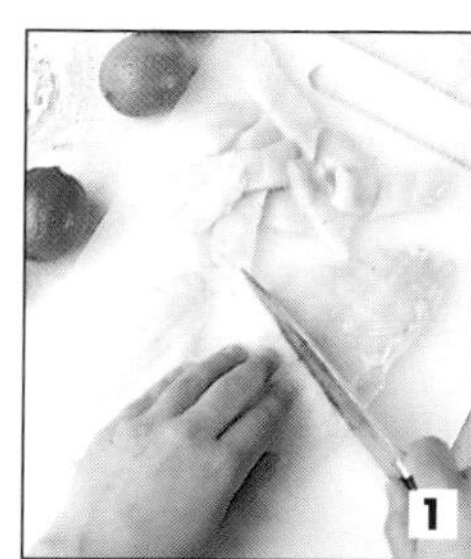

1

1 Lay each sole fillet, skin side down, on a chopping board. Hold the tail with one hand and a long, sharp knife in the other. Holding the knife firmly against the skin, work the flesh up and away to free it completely. Cut the skinned fillets diagonally into strips 25mm/1in wide. Squeeze the juice from the limes.

2 Put the fish in a non-metallic dish and cover with the lime juice. Cover and leave in the fridge for 6 - 8 hours, turning at least once.

3 Meanwhile, prepare the vegetables. Put the tomato in a bowl and cover with the boiling water. Leave for 2 minutes. Remove and, if the skins have not split, pierce with a fork or skewer. Peel away the skins before the tomatoes get too cold, cut into quarters and de-seed, then chop and put into a mixing bowl.

4 Wearing rubber gloves, de-seed and very finely chop the chilli, then add to the tomatoes. Finely chop the onion and add to the bowl. Stir in the oil, vinegar and chopped coriander and mix together.

5 Pour off the marinating juices from the fish and add to the vegetables. Add the fish to the bowl and stir together, taking care not to break up the fish. Transfer to a serving dish, garnish with a sprig of coriander and serve at once.

4

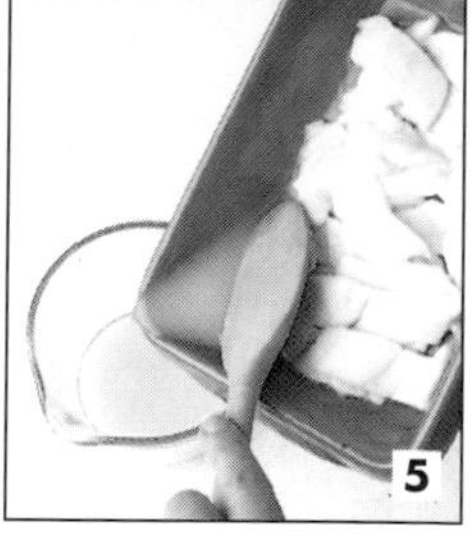

5

WHAT TO DRINK

Drink a chilled lager, or try a dry white wine such as Muscadet de Sèvre-et-Maine.

COOK'S TIPS

The lemon sole used in this dish is 'cooked' by marinating it in the lime juice. The acidity of the juice breaks down the muscle fibres of the fish and tenderizes the flesh. However, because the fish hasn't been cooked by exposing it to heat, which kills any bacteria present, you must ensure that you only use very fresh fish.

Baked Eggs Mexicana

THE HOT AND SPICY FLAVOURS OF MEXICAN COOKERY ADD PIQUANCY TO THIS QUICK AND COLOURFUL EGG DISH

SERVES 4

20 MINS TO PREPARE

30 MINS TO COOK

185 KCAL PER SERVING

SUITABLE FOR VEGETARIANS

2 tbls olive oil
1 onion, chopped
2 garlic cloves, crushed
400g / 14oz tin chopped tomatoes
½ red pepper, de-seeded and diced
2 courgettes, grated
1 tbls tomato purée
½ tsp chilli powder
hot pepper sauce
4 eggs
large pinch of paprika
sprig of flat-leaved parsley, to garnish (optional)

1 Heat the oven to 180°C/350°F/gas 4. Heat the oil in a saucepan over medium heat and add the onion and garlic. Fry for 5 minutes or until translucent, stirring frequently.

2 Stir in the tomatoes, red pepper, courgette, tomato purée, chilli powder and a dash of hot pepper sauce and stir well. Continue cooking for a further 15 minutes or until the mixture has thickened slightly. Spoon into a shallow ovenproof dish.

3 Mentally divide the vegetables in the dish into quarters. Make a dent in each quarter of the sauce with a spoon and carefully break an egg into it.

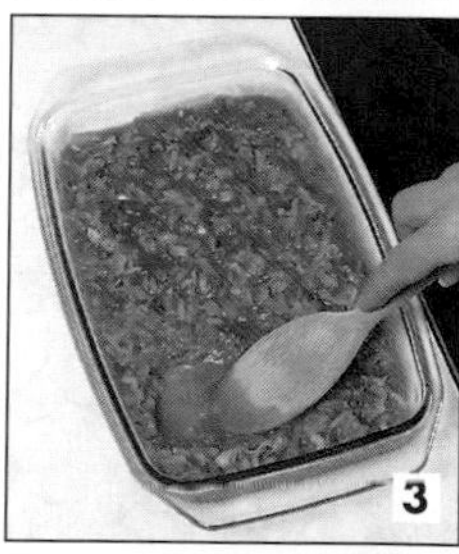

4 Continue until all the eggs have been broken into the vegetable mixture. Place in the oven and bake for 10 minutes or until the eggs are just set.

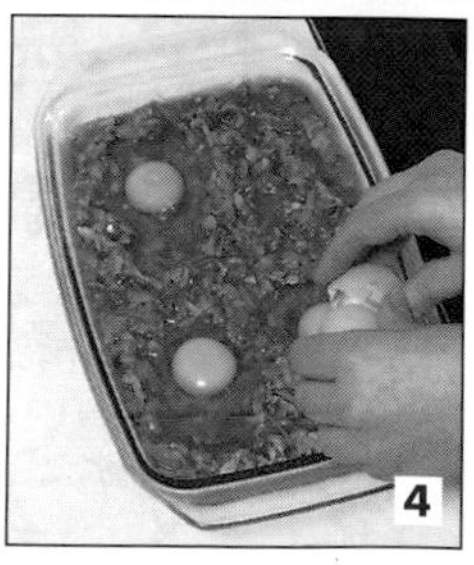

5 Sprinkle with the paprika and garnish with a sprig of parsley, if wished. Serve at once.

SERVING SUGGESTIONS

Eggs and Vegetables Mexicana makes a tasty light lunch or supper dish. Serve it with plain boiled rice or crusty French bread and a crisp green salad. If you're serving this for children or anyone who is not so keen on spicy food, simply omit the chilli and hot pepper sauce in step 2.

WHAT TO DRINK

Very spicy foods are hard to match with a wine. Try a light red wine such as a Spanish Tempranillo or a simple Beaujolais with this dish.

Easy Chilli con Carne

THIS EVER-POPULAR MEXICAN MINCED BEEF DISH IS PERFECT SERVED WITH PLAIN BOILED RICE OR AS A TOPPING FOR JACKET POTATOES

SERVES 4

15 MINS TO PREPARE

1 HR TO COOK

515 KCAL PER SERVING

2 tbls vegetable oil
1 large onion, finely chopped
1 green pepper, de-seeded and chopped
1 red pepper, de-seeded and chopped
2 tsp hot chilli powder
2 tsp ground cumin
600g / 1¼lb lean minced beef
2 tbls tomato purée
400g / 14oz tin chopped tomatoes
400g / 14oz tin red kidney beans, drained and rinsed
salt and pepper
275ml / ½ pt sour cream
snipped fresh chives to garnish, optional

1 Heat the oil in a large frying pan over medium heat. Add the onion and peppers and fry, stirring frequently, for 5 minutes or until softened but not browned. Stir in the chilli powder and cumin and continue to cook, stirring often, for 5 minutes.

2 Add the minced beef to the pan and mix with the other ingredients, using a spatula to break it up. Increase the heat to high and cook, stirring occasionally, for 5 - 8 minutes or until the meat is well browned. Spoon off any excess fat.

3 Add the tomato purée and stir until well blended. Stir in the tomatoes and the red kidney beans.

4 Bring the mixture to the boil, then reduce the heat to low. Partially cover the pan and simmer for 30 - 40 minutes or until the meat and vegetables are tender. Season with salt and pepper to taste. Pour the soured cream into a bowl and garnish with a sprinkling of chives, if liked; serve with the hot chilli.

WHAT TO DRINK

This strong-tasting dish needs a robust red wine such as a Navarra from Spain.

SERVING SUGGESTIONS

Chilli con Carne is an ideal dish for parties because it can be made a day ahead and reheated just before serving. Serve with a selection of toppings and let guests add their own, such as finely grated Cheddar cheese, plain Greek-style yogurt or finely diced avocado tossed with a little lemon juice. If you are feeding a large number of people on a tight budget, bulk out the meat with extra tinned beans and some frozen or tinned sweetcorn.

Pork & Chilli Casserole

THIS WARMING CASSEROLE TASTES EVEN BETTER REHEATED THE NEXT DAY. SERVE THE CASSEROLE ON A BED OF RICE TO COUNTERACT THE HEAT OF THE SPICES

SERVES 4

25 MINS TO PREPARE

1 HR 30 MINS TO COOK

385 KCAL PER SERVING

2 tbls olive oil
450g / 1lb lean shoulder pork steak, cut into 12mm / ½in cubes
2 onions, chopped
2 carrots, sliced
1 stick celery, chopped
1 clove garlic, crushed
½ level tsp hot chilli powder, optional
1 level tsp cumin seeds
650g / 23oz tinned chopped tomatoes
2 tbls tomato purée
425g / 15oz tinned red kidney beans in chilli sauce
fried cumin seeds, to garnish sour cream, to garnish

1 Heat the oven to 180°C / 350°F / gas 4. Heat the oil in a flameproof casserole. Add the pork, onions, carrots and celery and fry for 5 minutes, stirring occasionally.

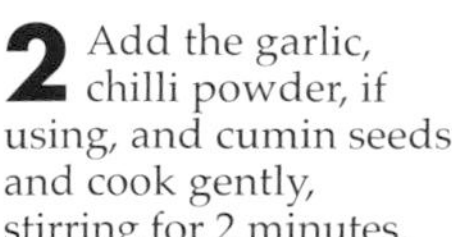

2 Add the garlic, chilli powder, if using, and cumin seeds and cook gently, stirring for 2 minutes.

3 Add the tinned tomatoes, tomato purée and kidney beans. Bring to the boil, stirring. Cover, transfer to the oven and cook for 1¼ - 1½ hours until the meat is tender, stirring occasionally.

4 Garnish the pork with fried cumin seeds and a spoonful of sour cream before serving.

VARIATIONS

If you like your chilli very hot, use plain drained kidney beans and add an extra half teaspoon of hot chilli powder to the casserole at step 2.

WHAT TO DRINK

This dish is quite hot and spicy, particularly if you like your chilli very hot and add extra chilli powder. A fresh young fruity red wine such as Côtes du Rhône would do well here, being very refreshing on the palate.

Peppered Pork with Chilli Salsa

TENDER PORK FILLETS, MARINATED WITH GARLIC AND CUMIN AND SERVED WITH A SPICY CHILLI SALSA, MAKE A SIMPLE BUT EFFECTIVE MAIN COURSE

SERVES 4

30 MINS TO PREPARE, PLUS MARINATING

40 MINS TO COOK

310 KCAL PER SERVING

700g / 1½lb pork fillet

for the marinade:
2 tbls olive oil
2 tsp white wine vinegar
2 garlic cloves, crushed
½ tsp ground cumin
1 tsp ground black pepper

for the salsa:
1 tbls olive oil
½ onion, finely chopped
1 - 2 green chillies, de-seeded and chopped
400g / 14oz tin chopped tomatoes
2 tbls tomato purée
150ml / 5fl oz chicken stock, made with 1 stock cube
1 tsp sugar
1 tsp ground cumin

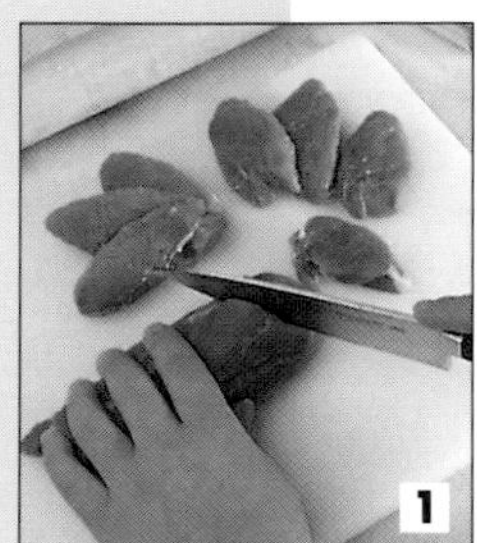
1

3

4

1 Cut the pork fillet diagonally into 12mm/½in slices.

2 Put each slice of fillet between two pieces of clingfilm and beat it gently with a rolling pin or meat tenderizer to make it slightly thinner.

3 To make the marinade, mix together the oil, vinegar, garlic, cumin and black pepper. Put the pork in a shallow, non-metallic dish. Add the marinade and coat well. Cover and leave to marinate in the fridge for at least 1 hour.

4 To make the salsa, heat the oil and fry the onion and chillies for 5 minutes or until soft. Add the rest of the ingredients and simmer for 20 - 30 minutes or until the salsa has thickened. Add salt and pepper to taste, if needed.

5 Remove the pieces of pork from the marinade and grill for about 3 minutes each side under a hot grill. Do this in two batches, if necessary. Serve immediately, with the chilli salsa.

WHAT TO DRINK

Try a young Côtes du Rhône. This fresh and fruity red wine goes well with this spicy pork dish.

COOK'S TIPS

The juices in chillies irritate the skin, so either wear rubber gloves when you cut them up, or wash your hands well after handling them. Never touch your eyes or face when handling chillies.

Tequila & Pineapple Delight

EXOTIC PINEAPPLE AND FIERY TEQUILA, TWO CLASSIC MEXICAN INGREDIENTS, ARE COMBINED WITH TRIFLE SPONGES AND CREAM TO MAKE A HEAVENLY DESSERT

SERVES
4

15 MINS
TO PREPARE

20 MINS
TO COOK

595 KCAL
PER
SERVING

SUITABLE
FOR
VEGETARIANS

1 small pineapple
4 tbls ground almonds
3 egg yolks
4 tbls sugar
3 tbls tequila
4 trifle sponges
3 tbls apricot jam
225ml / 8fl oz crème fraîche
50g / 2oz blanched almonds

1

2

3

1 Peel the pineapple and cut into quarters. Cut away the central core from each piece and discard. Finely chop the flesh and put into a saucepan. Add the ground almonds, egg yolks, sugar and 2 tbls tequila and place the pan over medium heat. Cook until the mixture thickens, stirring constantly. Transfer to a bowl and set aside to cool.

2 Cut the trifle sponges in half. Using 2 tbls apricot jam, spread jam over the cut side of each sponge half.

3 Cover the base of a serving dish with half the jam-covered sponges, overlapping them if necessary, and sprinkle ½ tbls tequila over them. Spoon half the pineapple mixture over the sponges. Add another layer of sponge halves, jam sides up, and sprinkle with the remaning tequila. Cover with the remaining pineapple mixture. Spread the crème fraîche over the top of the dessert.

4 Heat 1 tbls apricot jam with 1 tbls water in a small saucepan over low heat to make a thin syrup, stirring constantly. Drizzle this over the dessert, using a spoon to swirl it lightly into the cream.

5 Heat the grill to high. Place a piece of foil over the wire rack in the grill pan and sprinkle the almonds on evenly. Toast for 1 minute or until lightly browned, stirring and watching closely to make sure they do not burn. Leave to cool, then scatter over the top of the dessert.

INGREDIENTS GUIDE

Tequila is a clear spirit made in Mexico from a cactus-like plant called the agave. Juice is extracted, left to fement, then distilled to make a highly alcoholic drink. Tequila can be clear or a golden colour, depending on how it was aged. In Mexico, it is traditional to drink the tequila in one gulp, accompanied by a slice of lime and a pinch of salt. You can buy tequila in miniature bottles and there is enough in one for this dessert. If you can't get tequila, then substitute Cointreau or white rum.

Crème fraîche is a slightly acidic cream which originated in France. If you can't find any, use sour cream instead.

Mexican Caramel Custard

SILKEN CUSTARD, FLAVOURED WITH ORANGE, IS COATED WITH CARAMEL IN THIS TRADITIONAL DESSERT

SERVES 4

20 MINS TO PREPARE

45 MINS TO COOK, PLUS COOLING

340 KCAL PER SERVING

SUITABLE FOR VEGETARIANS

575ml / 1pt milk
175g / 6oz sugar
4 eggs
grated zest of 1 orange
hot water

1 Heat the milk and 50g/2oz sugar together until the sugar dissolves, then leave to cool. Beat the eggs well in a bowl and add the orange zest. Pour the sweetened milk into the eggs, whisking very thoroughly.

2 Heat the oven to 180°C/350°F/gas 4. To make the caramel, heat the remaining sugar in a dry saucepan until it dissolves and turns a rich golden brown. Don't stir, but swirl the pan around if necessary. Immediately it reaches the right shade – don't let it get too dark or it will taste bitter – remove from the heat and carefully stir in 2 tbls water. It will bubble up, so stand well back and take care.

3 Working quickly and holding the moulds with an oven glove or cloth, pour a little of the caramel into each mould, swirling it around to coat the sides.

4 Strain the custard and carefully fill the moulds. Stand them in a roasting tin or baking dish. Pour in enough hot water to come about halfway up the sides of the moulds and put the tin in the oven for about 30 minutes. To test, stick a small knife or skewer into the centre of a custard: if it comes out clean, the custard is done. Remove from the hot water, allow to cool, then chill.

5 Just before you serve the custards, turn them out by placing a small plate upside down on top of each mould. Invert carefully, holding the plate and mould together, then put the plate down and carefully lift off the mould.

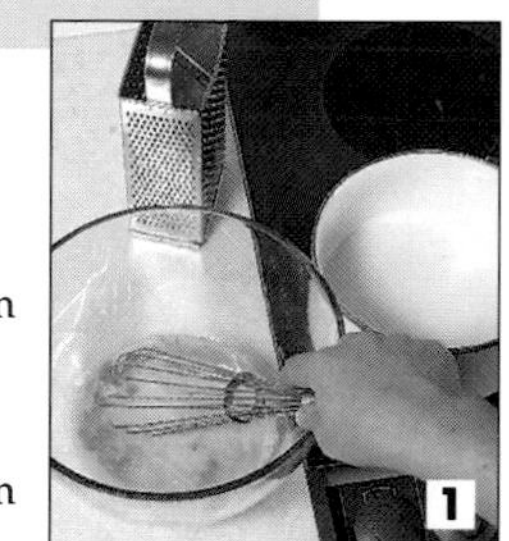

1

3

4

VARIATIONS

This dessert is also popular throughout Spain and Portugal and, in its most classic form, is flavoured with vanilla. There are many variations, however; as well as adding orange zest, as in this recipe, some recipes add a little shredded coconut, or a drop of coffee flavouring.

The Food of India

Each of the many regions of India has a wealth of herbs and spices and a diversity of local produce. This results in a variety of regional dishes, from the mild, fruit-based dishes of Kashmir to the myriad highly spiced fish dishes of Bengal.

Spices, seasonings and herbs are the vital core of Indian cooking. The most common are turmeric, coriander, cumin, chilli, fenugreek, ginger, garlic, mustard seeds, white poppy seeds, saffron and cardamom.

Indian cooks might use eight or ten spices for a particular dish. Commercially packaged curry powders are a handy substitute, but since they tend to impart the same flavour to every dish, it is worth buying the spices separately if possible.

Contents

Tandoori-spiced Prawn Kebabs

SUCCULENT TIGER PRAWNS, FLAVOURED WITH YOGURT, LEMON AND SPICES, ARE GRILLED TO PERFECTION IN THIS SIMPLE BUT DELICIOUS DISH

SERVES 4 - 8

25 MINS TO PREPARE, PLUS MARINATING

10 MINS TO COOK

120 KCAL PER SERVING

32 uncooked tiger prawns

for the marinade:
4 tbls yogurt
25mm / 1in cube fresh root ginger, peeled and grated
1 large garlic clove, crushed
4 tsp lemon juice
1½ tsp ground cumin
1½ tsp ground cinnamon
¼ tsp salt

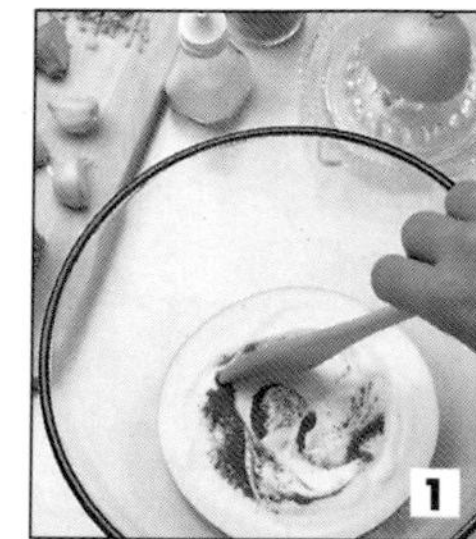

1

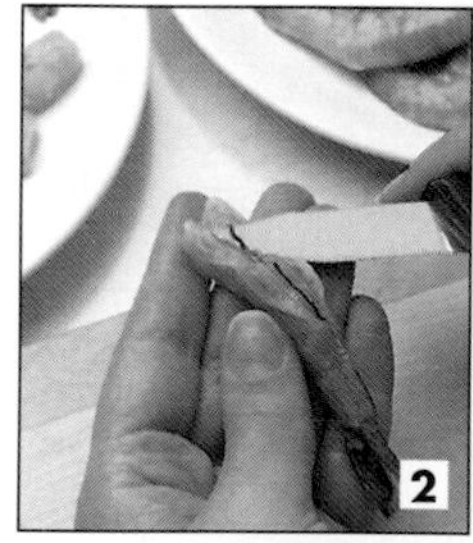

2

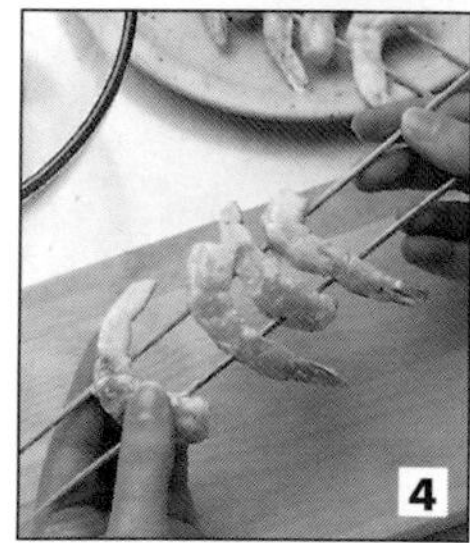

4

1 Combine all the marinade ingredients in a non-metallic bowl, mixing well.

2 Remove the shells from the prawns, but leave on the tail pieces. Carefully pick up the black vein that runs along the back of the prawn, pull it away and discard.

3 Stir the prepared prawns into the marinade, cover and leave in the fridge for at least 30 minutes; you can leave them to marinate for up to 4 hours.

4 Heat the grill to high. Remove the prawns from the marinade and thread eight prawns on two wooden barbecue skewers. Using two skewers makes it easier to turn the kebabs during cooking – this way the prawns will not spin around on the skewers. Continue in this way until you have used all the prawns.

5 Place the prawn kebabs under the grill and cook for 2 - 3 minutes on each side or until the flesh becomes pink and firm. Serve at once.

SERVING SUGGESTIONS

Four tiger prawns per person make an ideal light starter. For a main course, allow eight prawns per person and serve them with naan or pitta bread, some green salad and a bowl of mint and yogurt dip.

VARIATIONS

Why not serve this dish at your next barbecue? The marinade is easy to prepare and you need only leave the prawns to soak for as long as it takes to get the barbecue going. A few minutes over the coals and you will have a delicious treat for family and friends alike.

Curried Fish & Tomatoes

COOKED IN A MILD AND CREAMY SAUCE, THIS LIGHT FISH DISH IS AN IDEAL MAIN COURSE TO SERVE AT AN INDIAN-STYLE DINNER

SERVES 4

35 MINS TO PREPARE

1 HR 10 MINS TO COOK

345 KCAL PER SERVING

3 garlic cloves
25mm / 1in cube fresh root ginger, peeled
salt
1 tbls coriander seeds
1 tbls cumin seeds
350g / 12oz tomatoes
boiling water
2 tbls vegetable oil
1½ tsp ground fenugreek
1½ tsp ground turmeric
4 tbls double cream
275ml / ½pt Greek yogurt
2 tsp paprika
900g / 2lb filleted white fish (haddock or cod), in 4 pieces
pinch of cayenne pepper
1 tbls wine vinegar
thin slices of lime and chilli flowers, to garnish (optional)

1 Slice half the garlic and ginger; reserve. Using a pestle and mortar, pound the rest of the garlic and ginger to a paste with ½ tsp salt and reserve, then crush the coriander and cumin seeds.

2 Put the tomatoes in a bowl of boiling water for 2 minutes. Remove, peel away the skins, de-seed and chop. Drain in a sieve.

3 Heat the oil in a frying pan and fry the fenugreek over low heat for 2 minutes, stirring. Add the sliced ginger and garlic and, when these are golden, remove from the pan and reserve. Add the garlic paste, coriander, cumin, turmeric and tomatoes to the oil with 425ml / 15fl oz water. Bring to the boil, then lower the heat and simmer for 5 minutes.

4 Heat the oven to 200°C / 400°F / gas 6. Beat the cream and yogurt together well and add to the pan with the paprika and sliced garlic and ginger. Bring just to the boil, then lower the heat and simmer very gently for 20 minutes or until the sauce is reduced by about half.

5 Dust both sides of the fish with salt and cayenne pepper and sprinkle with vinegar, then put in a baking dish. Bake for 10 minutes, then drain off any liquid produced during cooking. Reduce the oven temperature to 180°C / 350°F / gas 4.

6 Pour the sauce over the fish. Bake for about 30 minutes or until tender. Garnish with lime slices and chilli flowers, if liked, and serve.

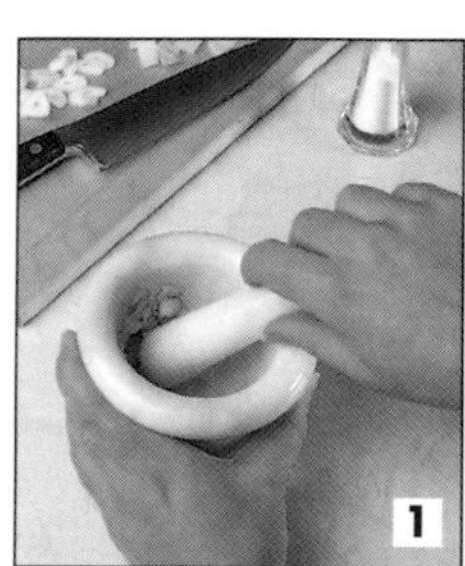
1

3

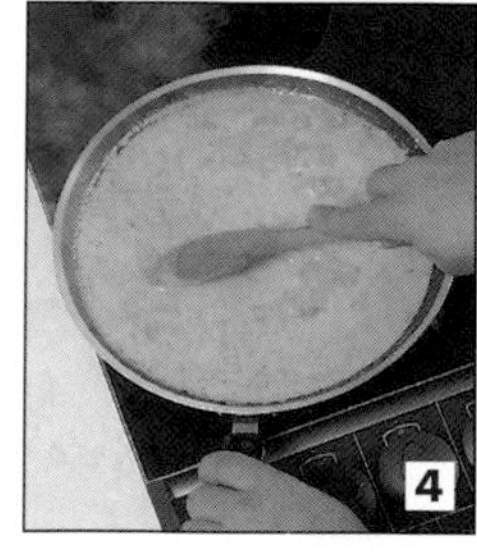
4

INGREDIENTS GUIDE

Fenugreek – also known as methi *in India – is a pungent spice which is used on its own in pickles and chutneys or combined with other spices to flavour vegetable dishes. The small brown seeds are usually lightly roasted before they are ground; you can buy it whole or powdered.*

Balti Chicken & Prawn Masala

WITH AN ABUNDANCE OF WONDERFULLY AROMATIC SPICES, THIS IS A GREAT ALTERNATIVE TO MORE USUAL CURRIES. HAVE YOUR BALTI SAUCE READY AND START STIR-FRYING!

SERVES 4 - 6

30 MINS TO PREPARE, PLUS MAKING SAUCE

20 MINS TO COOK

560 KCAL PER SERVING

4 tbls ghee or vegetable oil
2 garlic cloves, crushed
25mm / 1in cube fresh root ginger, peeled and finely chopped
1 tsp ground turmeric
1 tsp ground cumin
1 tsp ground coriander
1 tsp paprika
700g / 1½lb boneless, skinless chicken breasts, cut into 25mm / 1in cubes
1 large Spanish onion, chopped
2 tomatoes, chopped
1 recipe balti sauce (see below)
3 tbls chopped fresh coriander
1 green chilli, de-seeded and chopped
150ml / 5fl oz strained Greek yogurt
225g / ½lb peeled cooked tiger prawns
2 tsp garam masala
salt to taste
coriander sprigs, to garnish

1 First make the sauce, if you haven't already.

2 Heat the ghee or oil in a balti pan, wok or large, deep frying pan over high heat. Add the garlic, ginger, turmeric, cumin, ground coriander and paprika and stir-fry for 30 seconds. Add the chicken pieces, onion and tomatoes and stir-fry for 5 minutes or until the chicken is cooked through and the onions are golden.

3 Add the balti sauce, chopped coriander and green chilli. Mix well and bring to the boil. Reduce the heat to low and simmer gently for 10 minutes, stirring occasionally.

4 Add the yogurt, a tablespoon at a time, stirring well after each addition. Mix in the prawns, and sprinkle with the garam masala and salt to taste. Heat through gently for 2 - 3 minutes or until the prawns are piping hot. Garnish with coriander and serve at once.

COOK'S TIPS

To make a balti sauce, stir-fry 1½ chopped large Spanish onions in 2½ tbls ghee or vegetable oil until translucent. Add 2 chopped garlic cloves, 25mm (1in) peeled and chopped fresh root ginger, ¾ tsp each fenugreek seeds, ground coriander and cumin, ½ tsp each fennel seeds and turmeric and a pinch chilli powder. Add the seeds from 3 cardamom pods, 2½ pieces cassia bark and 1 - 2 cinnamon sticks, depending on the size, and stir together.

Add 200ml / 7fl oz stock or water, 3 chopped tomatoes and 2 bay leaves. Bring to the boil, then reduce the heat, cover and simmer for 25 minutes, stirring often. Discard the cassia and bay leaves, cool slightly and purée in a blender or food processor.

Lamb Tikka Chops

THIS MILDLY SPICED DISH, SERVED WITH INDIAN BREAD, MAKES A CHANGE FROM THE SKEWERED TIKKA KEBABS. CHOOSE THE CUT OF MEAT TO SUIT THE OCCASION – AND YOUR BUDGET

SERVES 4

20 MINS TO PREPARE

10 MINS TO COOK

260 KCAL PER SERVING

700g / 1½lb lamb chump chops

for the marinade:
150ml / ¼pt Greek yogurt
100ml / 3½fl oz freshly squeezed lemon juice (about 2 lemons)
2 cloves garlic, finely chopped
25mm / 1in piece fresh root ginger, grated
¼ tsp freshly ground black pepper
½ - 1 tsp ground cumin
½ tsp chilli powder
1 tsp garam masala
pinch ground nutmeg
pinch ground cloves
1 tbls finely chopped fresh mint
1 - 2 tbls freshly chopped fresh coriander

for the garnish:
1 lemon, cut in wedges
2 tomatoes, cut in slices
a few sprigs of coriander
sliced red onions

1 Put the chops in a shallow dish. Put the yogurt and lemon juice into a bowl and whisk. Add the remaining marinade ingredients and mix.

2 Spoon the marinade over the lamb and toss well. Cover tightly and put in the fridge to marinate for at least 2 hours and preferably overnight. Stir the mixture occasionally.

3 Remove the lamb chops from the fridge 30 minutes before cooking so that they have time to reach room temperature before cooking.

4 Remove the chops from the marinade and put them in a griddle pan over high heat, or on the grilling rack under a hot grill. Cook for 1 minute on each side. Lower the heat and cook for 5 minutes on each side.

5 Place on a serving dish. Garnish with lemon, tomato, sprigs of coriander, and onion.

SERVING SUGGESTIONS

Serve these spicy chops with hot naan bread, chapaties or pitta bread and salad.

COOK'S TIP

The same marinade can be used for lamb tikka kebabs or for chicken kebabs. If you grill these on a griddle pan it is easy to judge how fast they are cooking.

Spicy Aubergine Curry

THE SOFT TEXTURE OF AUBERGINES, COUPLED WITH A SPICY, OILY SAUCE, MAKES A VEGETARIAN DISH THAT IS HEARTY ENOUGH TO SERVE AS A MAIN COURSE

SERVES 4 - 6

20 MINS TO PREPARE PLUS STANDING

50 MINS TO COOK

265 KCAL PER SERVING

SUITABLE FOR VEGETARIANS

2 large aubergines
salt
8 tbls sunflower oil
1 medium onion, chopped
2 garlic cloves, crushed and chopped
25mm / 1in cube of fresh root ginger, roughly chopped
1 tbls ground coriander
½ tbls ground cumin
1 tsp ground turmeric
1 dried red chilli pepper, crushed finely
1 tsp black mustard seeds
4 cardamom pods, gently crushed
125ml / 4fl oz vegetable stock (made with a cube if necessary)
fresh coriander leaves, to garnish
lemon wedges, to garnish

1

1 Cut the aubergines into cubes about 4cm/1½in square. Place in a colander, sprinkle generously with salt and cover with a plate. Leave to stand so that the excess water seeps out.

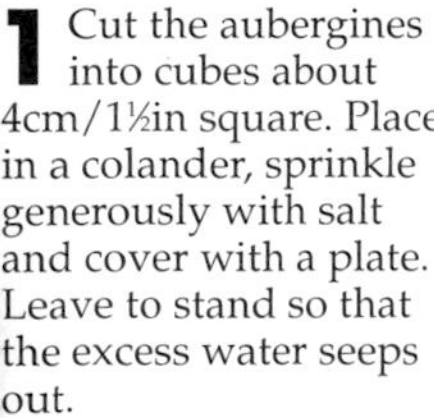

2 Heat 2 tbls of the oil in a heavy-based saucepan over medium-high heat and fry the aubergines, in batches, so that they are browned on all sides. Remove to drain on kitchen towel as you cook them. Add more oil to the pan between batches if necessary.

3 Put the remaining ingredients, apart from the cardamom pods, stock and fresh coriander, in a food processor or blender and pulverize them. Put the remaining oil in a pan, add the onion and spice mixture and cook for about 5 minutes, stirring constantly.

2

4 Add the stock to the spice mixture, stirring as you add it. Bring to the boil and add the aubergines. Partially cover the pan and simmer for 15 - 20 minutes. Transfer to a warm serving dish and garnish with fresh coriander and lemon.

4

SERVING SUGGESTIONS

Serve this dish with rice and peas for a balanced vegetarian meal. Alternatively, it makes a juicy accompaniment to dry meat dishes, such as Lamb Tikka Chops.

Spinach, Mushroom & Red Pepper Balti

THIS COLOURFUL VEGETABLE DISH IS DELICIOUSLY SPICY AND FULL OF INTERESTING TEXTURES. IF YOU MAKE THE BALTI SAUCE IN ADVANCE, THE DISH IS QUICK AND EASY TO COOK

SERVES 4 - 6

35 MINS TO PREPARE, PLUS MAKING SAUCE

25 MINS TO COOK

360 KCAL PER SERVING

SUITABLE FOR VEGETARIANS

1 recipe balti sauce (see p39)
700g / 1½lb spinach, stalks removed
2 potatoes, peeled and cut into bite-sized pieces
salt
boiling water
4 tbls ghee or vegetable oil
1 tsp cumin seeds
1 tsp fenugreek seeds
1 tsp ground turmeric
2 tsp garam masala
¼ - ½ tsp chilli powder
1 onion, quartered and thinly sliced
2 garlic cloves, crushed
1 large red pepper, de-seeded and cut into 6mm / ¼in strips
450g / 1lb button mushrooms

1 First make the sauce, if you haven't already.

2 Place the spinach in a large saucepan with only the water clinging to the leaves. Cover and cook over medium heat for 5 minutes or until it is wilted, turning frequently. Drain well in a colander, pressing firmly with a back of a spoon to extract as much liquid as possible. Cook the potatoes in a pan of salted boiling water for about 8 minutes or until just tender. Drain well.

3 Heat the ghee or oil in a balti pan, wok or large, deep frying pan over medium heat. Add the spices and stir-fry for 30 seconds. Add the onion, garlic and red pepper and stir-fry for 2 minutes. Add the mushrooms and continue stir-frying for a further 2 - 3 minutes.

4 Stir in the potato pieces, spinach, salt to taste and the prepared balti sauce, using two forks to separate any thick clumps of spinach leaves. Cook gently for 3 minutes or until heated through. Transfer to a serving dish and serve hot.

WHAT TO DRINK

Red wine goes well with spicy foods, so try a young Beaujolais with this balti dish. However, if you don't want to drink wine, then a chilled Indian lager or a pilsner beer would be ideal.

COOK'S TIPS

The cooked spinach may be coarsely chopped, if wished, although the appearance is better if left as whole leaf spinach. Make sure that the spinach is thoroughly drained after cooking or the excess liquid will make the consistency of the finished dish rather thin and watery.

To speed up the cooking process for future balti meals, why not make up double the quantity of Balti sauce in advance and freeze what you don't need now, ready to use when required?

Spicy Potato & Pea Bhaji

IN THIS INDIAN VEGETABLE DISH, POTATOES AND PEAS ARE GIVEN A REAL LIFT WITH A HOT GREEN CHILLI AND CURRY SPICES

SERVES 4

20 MINS TO PREPARE

35 MINS TO COOK

255 KCAL PER SERVING

SUITABLE FOR VEGETARIANS

1 green chilli
3 - 4 tbls vegetable oil
1 onion, thinly sliced
1 tsp ground turmeric
1 tsp cumin seeds
¼ tsp ground ginger
450g / 1lb potatoes, peeled and diced
225g / ½lb frozen peas
2 tbls chopped fresh coriander

1 Heat the oven to 180°C/350°F/gas 4. Wearing rubber gloves, slit the chilli in half lengthways. Use a teaspoon to scoop out the seeds and discard them. Finely chop the chilli, removing and discarding the white membrane; set the chilli aside.

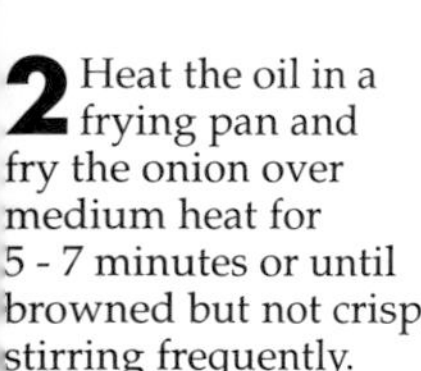

2 Heat the oil in a frying pan and fry the onion over medium heat for 5 - 7 minutes or until browned but not crisp, stirring frequently.

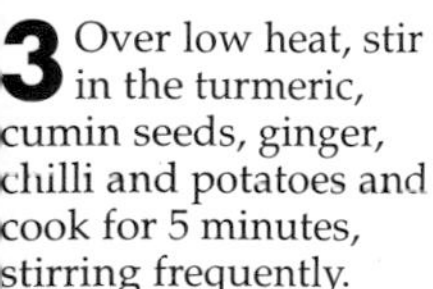

3 Over low heat, stir in the turmeric, cumin seeds, ginger, chilli and potatoes and cook for 5 minutes, stirring frequently.

4 Transfer the onion and potato mixture to a casserole, add the frozen peas and stir well. Cover and bake for 15 - 20 minutes or until the potatoes are tender.

5 To serve, turn the bhaji into a serving dish, garnish with the chopped coriander and serve hot.

COOK'S TIPS

Wear rubber gloves when you are handling chillies as their juices irritate the skin. Avoid any contact with your eyes and wash the knife and chopping board after use.

INGREDIENTS GUIDE

As a general rule, red chillies tend to be 'sweeter' than green ones, and the darker a green chilli is, the hotter it will be. Thin, pointed chillies tend to be hotter than short, rounded ones. However, despite these guidelines, there are exceptions and some chillies can be surprisingly hot.

When preparing them, bear in mind that the tip of the chilli is the mildest part and the seeds are the hottest.

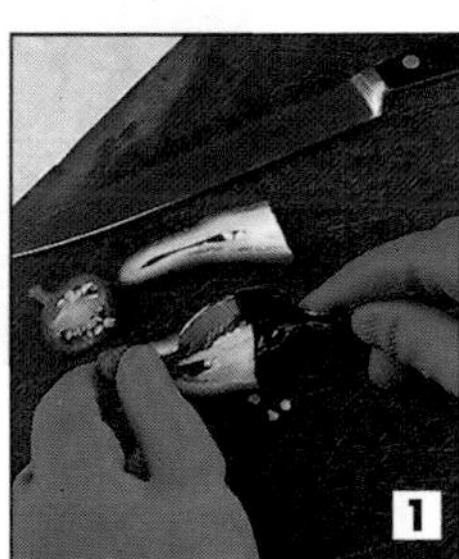

VARIATIONS

This dish is also very good made with chickpeas instead of green peas. Substitute the same amount of cooked or canned chickpeas and add to the pan towards the end of cooking time, just to heat them through.

Channa Dhal with Peppers

THIS COLOURFUL GUJERATI DISH HAS A MELLOW, SWEETISH FLAVOUR AND IS NOT AT ALL HOT. SERVE IT ON ITS OWN WITH BREAD OR RICE, OR SERVE IT AS A SIDE DISH AS PART OF A MORE ELABORATE MEAL

SERVES 4 - 6

25 MINS TO PREPARE PLUS SOAKING

1 HR 10 MINS TO COOK

325 KCAL PER SERVING

SUITABLE FOR VEGETARIANS

4 tbls vegetable oil
1 tsp mustard seeds
½ tsp cumin seeds
¼ tsp asafoetida (optional)
1 onion, finely chopped
3 garlic cloves, crushed
2 tsp ground cumin
seeds from 5 cardamom pods, crushed
½ tsp ground turmeric
1½ tsp salt
1 tsp sugar
2 tomatoes, skinned and chopped
225g / 8oz channa dhal, washed and soaked for at least 2 hours
850ml / 1½ pt boiling water
1 red pepper, de-seeded and diced
1 green pepper, de-seeded and diced
fresh coriander leaves, to garnish

1 Heat the oil in a large, heavy-based saucepan. Add the mustard and cumin seeds and the asafoetida, if using, and stir-fry gently until the seeds begin to pop. Add the onion and fry gently for a further 5 - 7 minutes until it turns golden.

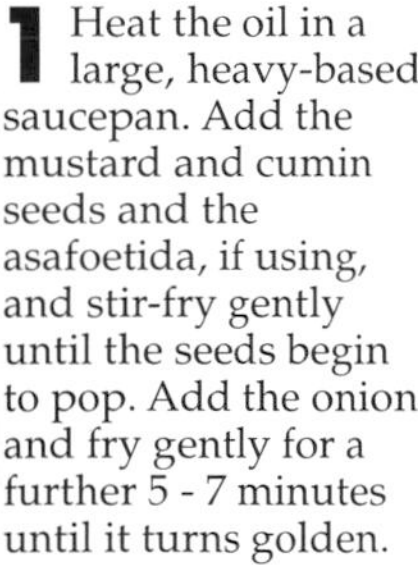

2 Add the garlic, ground cumin, cardamom and turmeric. Stir for 1 minute, then add the salt, sugar and tomatoes. Cook for a further 2 minutes, stirring frequently.

3 Drain the channa dhal and add to the pan with the boiling water. Bring the water back to the boil, then simmer over low heat for about 45 minutes.

4 When the dhal is soft and most of the water has been absorbed, mash gently with the back of a wooden spoon so that it breaks down and thickens the liquid.

5 Add the peppers and simmer for 10 minutes. Turn into a serving dish and garnish with coriander before serving.

COOK'S TIPS

The precise cooking time depends on the age of the dhal. It is ready when the dhal are just soft and the remaining liquid is thick and soupy. This dish should not be too dry.

INGREDIENTS GUIDE

Channa dhal are yellow split peas, readily available in most supermarkets and health food shops. They benefit from soaking for at least 2 hours before cooking, or overnight.

Spiced Gujerati Bread

MADE IN MINUTES, THIS FRAGRANTLY SPICED GUJERATI BREAD CALLED THEPLA IS PERFECT WITH DIPS OR FOR MOPPING UP TASTY JUICES FROM LENTILS OR OTHER CURRIED DISHES

MAKES 6

20 MINS TO PREPARE

10 MINS TO COOK

210 KCAL PER SERVING

SUITABLE FOR VEGETARIANS

175g / 6oz strong wholemeal flour
50g / 2oz chickpea flour
1 tsp chilli powder
¼ tsp ground turmeric
2 tsp dhana jeera powder (see Ingredients Guide)
3 tbls cooked rice
20mm / ¾in cube fresh root ginger, peeled and grated
1 tbls chopped fresh coriander
2 tsp sesame seeds
4 tbls groundnut oil
125ml / 4fl oz tepid water
oil for greasing

1

1 Sift the flours, chilli powder, turmeric and dhana jeera powder into a large bowl. Add the cooked rice, ginger, coriander, sesame seeds and 2 tbls of the oil and mix well.

2 Stir in the water and mix to a dough. Turn the dough out on to a lightly floured work surface and knead well for 3 minutes.

3 Put a few drops of oil in a heavy-based frying pan and put over a medium-high heat. Divide the dough into 6 balls, then roll one ball out on a lightly floured surface to an 18cm/7in-diameter circle. Put the thepla in the frying pan and fry for 30 - 45 seconds on each side.

4 Add a little more oil to the pan and fry for a few more seconds on each side until the thepla is flecked with brown. Put the cooked thepla in a basket and cover with a dry cloth to keep it warm while you roll out and cook the remaining dough in the same way.

3

4

INGREDIENTS GUIDE

- *Chickpea flour is often called gram flour. Look for it in good health food shops or Asian supermarkets.*
- *Dhana jeera powder is used extensively in Gujerati cooking. To make your own, dry-fry 4 tbls coriander seeds and 1 tbls cumin seeds separately in a preheated, heavy-based pan for 2 - 3 minutes. When fragrant remove from the pan immediately. Grind the seeds together to a fine powder. Keep any unused powder in a screw-top jar.*

COOK'S TIPS

Keep the dough covered with a clean damp cloth as you work in order to prevent it drying out.

Mango & Cardamom Kulfi

THIS DELICIOUS, EXOTIC DESSERT MADE WITH MANGOES AND FLAVOURED WITH CARDAMOM IS WONDERFULLY REFRESHING AFTER A SPICY MEAL

SERVES 4

20 MINS TO PREPARE, PLUS FREEZING

1 HR TO COOK

280 KCAL PER SERVING

2 HRS TO FREEZE

SUITABLE FOR VEGETARIANS

4 green cardamom pods
575ml / 1pt milk
2 tbls caster sugar
850g / 30oz tinned mango slices in syrup, drained
fresh mango slices and mint leaves, to decorate (optional)

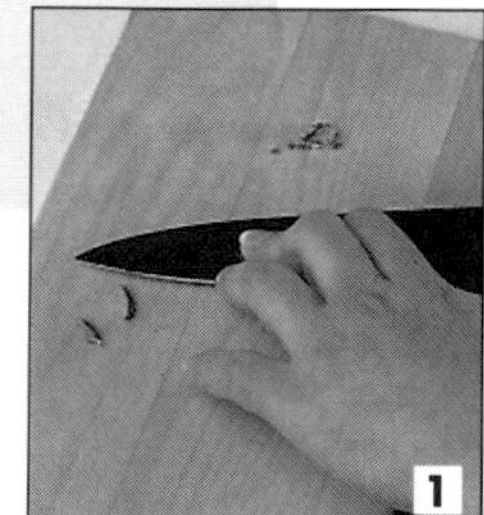
1

1 Crush the cardamom pods slightly, using the flat side of a knife blade or a mortar and pestle. Extract the brown seeds and put them into a heavy saucepan with the milk.

2

2 Bring just to the boil over medium heat, then lower the heat and simmer very gently for at least an hour, stirring frequently, until the milk is reduced to just over half. A skin will keep forming on the top; just stir it in.

3 Remove from the heat. Though they are edible, the cardamom seeds may be removed at this stage by straining the milk through a sieve, if you prefer. Make sure you press any milk skin through the sieve using the back of a spoon. Add the sugar and mango flesh and blend or process until smooth. Leave the mixture to cool.

4 Pour the mixture into individual moulds, cover with foil and freeze for 2 hours or until solid.

5 About 15 minutes before serving, transfer the kulfis from the freezer to the fridge to soften slightly. If the frozen mixture has risen in the middle, level it off with a sharp knife. To serve, dip each mould briefly into hot water and invert carefully on to a serving plate. Decorate with mango slices and mint leaves, if wished, and serve at once.

5

INGREDIENTS GUIDE

It is necessary to use whole milk for this recipe; low-fat milk will not reduce in the same way.

TOOLS OF THE TRADE

Kulfi is traditionally made in individual moulds. Specialist kulfi moulds – about 10cm/4in tall, almost conical in shape and made of aluminium – are available, though dariole moulds make perfect substitutes.

If you don't have either of these, use 150ml/5fl oz yogurt pots instead. Just make sure you wash them thoroughly before using them.

Layered Mango Crunch

THE INDIAN NAME FOR THIS PRETTY DESSERT IS MANGO SHRIKAND. IT'S A REFRESHING BLEND OF CURD CHEESE, YOGURT AND FRUIT

SERVES 4

30 MINS TO PREPARE, PLUS CHILLING

5 MINS TO COOK

405 KCAL PER SERVING

SUITABLE FOR VEGETARIANS

2 ripe mangoes	**350g / 12fl oz Greek yogurt**
4 cardamom pods	**50g / 2oz blanched almonds, toasted and chopped**
finely grated zest and juice of 1 lime	**mint sprigs, to decorate**
3 tbls caster sugar	
3 pieces cassia bark	
225g / ½lb curd cheese	

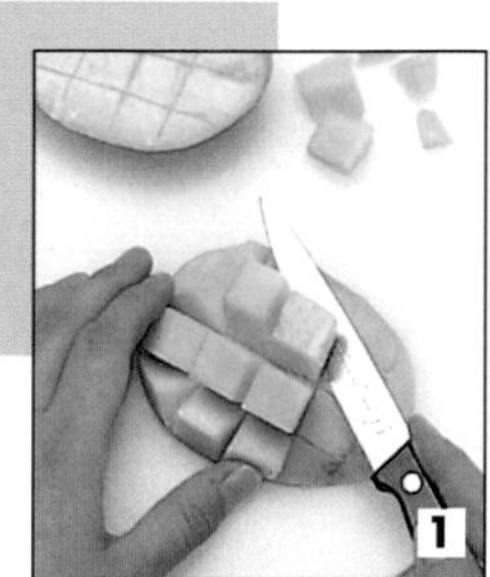
1

1 Stand a mango upright, narrow side facing you. Make two downward cuts on either side of the stone so that you end up with three pieces: two fleshy 'cheeks' and a central piece surrounding the stone. Slash the cut sides of each cheek in a grid pattern, going as far as the skin but not cutting through it, then turn inside out so that the cubes of flesh splay out. Cut them away from the skin. Remove the flesh surrounding the stone as best you can and place in a blender or food processor. Discard the skin. Repeat with the other mango.

2 Put half the cubes of mango into the blender, purée until smooth, then transfer to a large bowl. Set aside 1 tbls purée and add the remaining puréed mango to the mango cubes.

3 Crush the cardamom pods lightly and place in a small saucepan with the lime zest and juice, 1 tbls sugar and the cassia bark. Place over low heat for a few minutes or until hot, stirring frequently. Leave to cool. Strain and add to the mango cubes and purée; mix lightly.

3

4 Place the curd cheese, yogurt and remaining sugar in a bowl and mix until smooth. Stir in the reserved mango purée and mix well.

5 Place 2 tbls mango mixture in the bottom of a stemmed glass. Put some of the cheese mixture on top and sprinkle with a few almonds. Continue making layers, ending with a few almonds. Repeat in another three glasses. Chill for several hours and decorate with mint before serving.

5

CALORIE COUNTER

Reduce the calorie count in this recipe by using low-fat natural yogurt instead of the rich and creamy Greek type.

INGREDIENTS GUIDE

Mangoes are available all year round. When choosing, test for ripeness by cupping the fruit in your hand and squeezing gently – it should 'give' slightly to the touch when the fruit is ready for eating.

If you can't find cassia bark, substitute 2 cinnamon sticks.

The Food of the Middle East

The cuisine of Turkey has widespread origins. Nomadic tribes from Central Asia contributed a love of grilled meats, unleavened bread and fermented milk products, while rare spices arrived from the far reaches of the Ottoman Empire.

Creating a Moroccan meal at home need not be too time-consuming. One dish, such as the delicious lamb and vegetable couscous, will give you a taste of some of the exotic flavours of the country.

In the Lebanon poultry regularly appears on the table, often cooked in unusual ways, such as with a pine nut sauce. The bright, clean flavours of the food come from the generous use of herbs such as flat-leaved parsley, fresh coriander and thyme.

Contents

Middle Eastern Lentil Soup

GROUND CUMIN ADDS A SUBTLE, EXOTIC FLAVOUR TO THIS HEARTY SOUP THAT MAKES AN IDEAL FIRST COURSE TO SERVE BEFORE KEBABS OR ROAST LAMB

SERVES 6

10 MINS TO PREPARE

45 MINS TO COOK

210 KCAL PER SERVING

3 tbls olive oil
1 onion, finely chopped
275g / 10oz split red lentils, rinsed
1.4L / 2½pt beef stock
3 - 4 garlic cloves, finely chopped
2 tsp ground cumin
salt and pepper
6 tbls plain yogurt, to garnish (optional)
paprika, to garnish (optional)

2

3

4

1 Heat 2 tbls oil in a large saucepan and fry the onion over medium heat for 10 minutes until lightly browned, stirring frequently.

2 Add the lentils and stock and bring to the boil, then cover, lower the heat and simmer for 20 minutes or until the lentils are tender.

3 Meanwhile, heat the remaining oil in a small frying pan and fry the garlic over medium heat until it begins to brown, stirring frequently. Stir in the cumin, then remove from the heat.

4 Stir the garlic, cumin and any of the oil left in the pan into the lentils. Simmer for a further 15 minutes, then season to taste.

5 To serve, ladle the soup into six bowls. Swirl 1 tbls yogurt into each bowl and sprinkle with paprika, if wished.

VEGETARIAN OPTIONS

To make this filling soup suitable for a vegetarian meal, make it with vegetable rather than beef stock. If you serve the soup with a bread roll, it will be high in first-class protein.

INGREDIENTS GUIDE

Lentils, a type of dried pulse, are a popular ingredient throughout the Middle East, where they are often combined with grains to produce protein-rich vegetarian meals. We have used red lentils in this recipe, but you can also use yellow, green or brown lentils. Most pulses require lengthy soaking and boiling before long, slow cooking, but lentils are much quicker to use, as they are ready to cook when you buy them.

Persian Aubergine Dip

KNOWN AS *MELITZANOSALATA*, OR AUBERGINE SALAD, THIS IS AN IDEAL DIP TO SERVE WITH PITTA BREAD AS A STARTER, SNACK OR PARTY CENTREPIECE

SERVES 4 - 6

20 MINS TO PREPARE, PLUS CHILLIING

20 MINS TO COOK

100 KCAL PER SERVING

SUITABLE FOR VEGETARIANS

2 large or 3 medium aubergines
3 tbls olive oil
1 garlic clove, crushed
juice of 1 lemon
1 tbls tahini
1 tsp ground cumin
salt and pepper
olive and flat-leaved parsley, to garnish (optional)

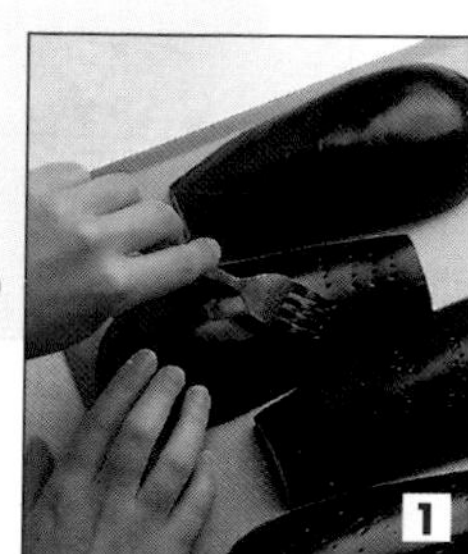

1

2

3

1 Heat the grill to high. Cut the aubergines in half lengthways. Grease a baking sheet with 1 tbls of the oil and place the aubergines on it, cut sides down. Prick the skins all over with a fork and grill for about 20 minutes or until the skins are wrinkled and the flesh feels soft. Keep checking while the aubergines are grilling to make sure they do not burn.

2 Remove the aubergines from the grill and allow them to cool slightly. When they are cool enough to handle, scoop out the flesh with a spoon – it should come away cleanly. Discard the skins.

3 Put the flesh in a blender or food processor and add the garlic, lemon juice, tahini, cumin and 1 tbls oil, then blend to a smooth purée. Taste, and add salt and pepper if necessary. Turn into a serving bowl and chill, covered, until ready to serve.

4 Remove from the fridge just before serving and trickle the remaining olive oil over the top. Garnish with an olive and flat-leaved parsley, if wished.

WHAT TO DRINK

Aubergine, garlic and tahini give this dip a rich and smoky flavour. It needs a fairly stong red wine to stand up to it, so go for Othello, a Californian Zinfandel or a Côtes du Rhône.

SERVING SUGGESTIONS

Warm pitta bread or an Indian bread such as naan would be ideal accompaniments for this tasty starter. Alternatively, you could serve crudités.

As a dinner-party starter this recipe will serve 4 - 6 people, but as part of a buffet it will serve at least 12 people.

INGREDIENTS GUIDE

Tahini, a thick, oily paste of ground sesame seeds, lends a unique nutty flavour to this dip. It keeps well in the fridge and can be used in other Middle Eastern recipes such as the chickpea dip known as hummus.

Roast Spiced Peppers

SOFT, JUICY PEPPERS FILLED WITH BULGUR WHEAT AND SERVED WITH A SPICY SALAD DRESSING MAKE A TASTY VEGETARIAN MAIN COURSE

SERVES 4

25 MINS TO PREPARE, PLUS SOAKING

45 MINS TO COOK

550 KCAL PER SERVING

SUITABLE FOR VEGETARIANS

100g / 4oz bulgur wheat
boiling water
2 red peppers
2 yellow peppers
2 tbls olive oil, plus extra for greasing
175g / 6oz tomatoes
2 onions, chopped
2 garlic cloves, finely chopped
50g / 2oz unsalted roasted cashew nuts, chopped
2 tbls chopped fresh mint
2 tbls chopped parsley
salt and pepper
lemon and lime wedges and salad leaves, to garnish

for the dressing:
125ml / 4fl oz olive oil
¼ - ½ tsp cayenne pepper, or to taste
2 tbls ground cumin
2 tbls tomato purée
juice of 2 limes

2

5

1 Heat the oven to 200°C/400°F/gas 6. Put the bulgur wheat in a large bowl and cover with boiling water. Leave to soak for 30 minutes or until tender, then drain well.

2 Meanwhile, halve the peppers lengthways and remove cores and seeds. Place, cut sides down, on a lightly oiled baking sheet and roast for 20 minutes or until they are softened and the edges have browned, turning the peppers over halfway through.

3 Put the tomatoes in a bowl, cover with boiling water and leave for 2 minutes. Remove and, if the skins have not split, pierce with a fork or skewer. Peel away the skins, cut in half, remove and discard the seeds, then chop the flesh.

4 Heat the oil in a large saucepan over medium heat. Fry the onions and garlic for 5 minutes or until soft, stirring frequently. Add the chopped tomatoes, cashew nuts, drained bulgur, mint, parsley and salt and pepper to taste. Cook, stirring often, for 1 - 2 minutes.

5 With a spoon, stuff the peppers with the bulgur mixture and return to the oven for 15 minutes or until heated through.

6 Meanwhile, whisk together the dressing ingredients in a small bowl, adding salt to taste. Arrange one red and one yellow pepper half on each plate and drizzle with a little of the dressing. Garnish with citrus wedges and salad. Transfer the remaining dressing to a small jug and serve separately.

VARIATIONS

Instead of using bulgur, you can use long-grain white or brown rice. Cook according to the instructions on the packet.

Chicken Wings with Pine Nut Sauce

JUICY CHICKEN WINGS ARE SPIKED WITH LEMON AND GARLIC, GRILLED UNTIL CRISP, AND THEN SERVED WITH A CREAMY SAUCE AND A GARNISH OF LIME WEDGES IN THIS CLASSIC LEBANESE MEZZE DISH

SERVES 6

20 MINS TO PREPARE, PLUS MARINATING

30 MINS TO COOK

480 KCAL PER SERVING

12 chicken wings, tips removed

for the marinade:
6 garlic cloves, crushed
5 tbls olive oil
juice of 1 large lemon
2 tsp paprika
1 tsp ground cumin
½ tsp crushed allspice berries
¼ tsp cayenne pepper
⅛ tsp cinnamon
salt and freshly ground black pepper

for the sauce:
225g / ½lb pine nuts, finely chopped
2 slices bread, crusts removed, soaked in water
juice of 3 lemons
2 garlic cloves, crushed
½ tsp salt

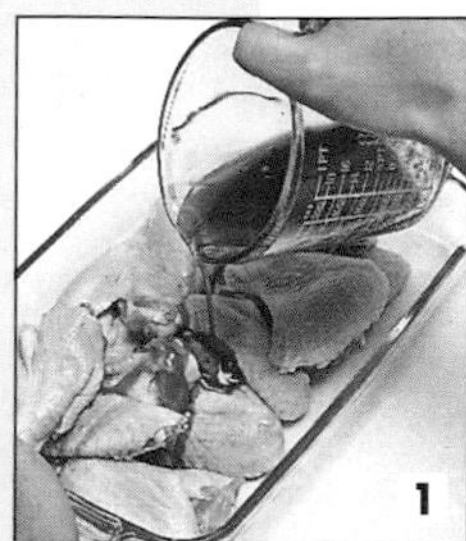
1

2

5

1 Put the chicken wings in a shallow dish. Combine the ingredients for the marinade in a jug and pour over the chicken. Cover and leave to marinate in the fridge for at least 2 hours or overnight.

2 Remove the chicken from the marinade and leave to return to room temperature. To make the sauce, put the pine nuts in a food processor or blender. Squeeze the bread dry and add to the nuts with all the remaining sauce ingredients.

3 Blend the nut mixture until it forms a smooth, creamy sauce, diluting it with a little water if it becomes too thick.

4 Grill the chicken wings under a medium grill for 20 - 30 minutes or until cooked through and slightly charred on the outside.

5 Transfer the chicken to a warm serving dish and garnish with lime wedges. Serve immediately with the sauce served separately in a bowl.

PLAN AHEAD

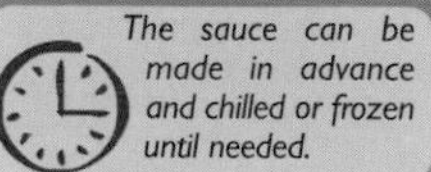

The sauce can be made in advance and chilled or frozen until needed.

SERVING SUGGESTIONS

Serve with warm pitta bread, using the extra sauce as a dip. Use yogurt instead of the sauce if you are short of time.

Kofte with Lemon & Coriander Sauce

LAMB FILLET IS GROUND TO A PASTE, MIXED WITH SPICES AND THEN GRILLED ON SKEWERS TO PRODUCE THESE SUCCULENT TURKISH KEBABS

SERVES 4 - 6

15MINS TO PREPARE

10 MINS TO COOK

482 KCAL PER SERVING

2 eggs, beaten
900g / 2lb lamb fillet, cubed
½ tsp ground coriander
½ tsp ground cumin
1 garlic clove, crushed
1 onion, roughly chopped
½ tsp salt
handful of fresh chopped coriander

for the lemon & coriander sauce:
4 egg yolks
4 tbls lemon juice
225ml / 8fl oz water
25g / 1oz fresh coriander leaves, chopped

1

1 Keeping the eggs aside, put all the remaining kebab ingredients in a food processor or blender and mix to a smooth paste. Remove the paste from the blender and gradually mix in the beaten eggs. Knead the mixture with your hands until it forms a pliable dough.

2 Dampen your hands so that the meat mixture doesn't stick to them, then break off egg-sized portions of the mixture and slip two portions on to each skewer.

3 Mould each portion of meat paste along the skewer to form a sausage shape. Heat the grill, and oil the grill pan. Place the kebabs in the grill pan and cook for 10 minutes under high heat until well browned, turning the skewers frequently.

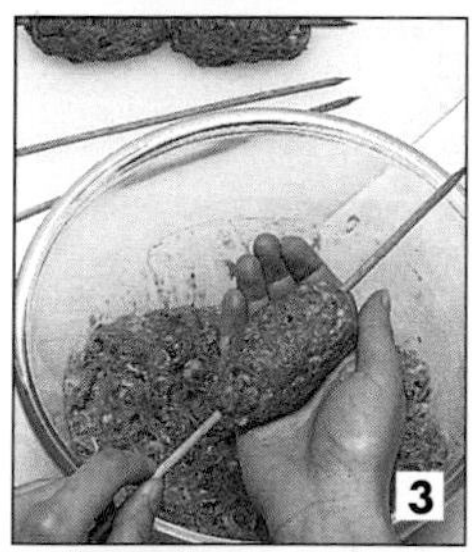
3

4 Meanwhile, make the sauce. Whisk the egg yolks in a heatproof bowl until pale and fluffy. Whisk in the lemon juice and water and blend together well.

5 Place the bowl over a saucepan of gently simmering water and stir the mixture until it thickens, without boiling. Stir in the chopped coriander leaves and serve immediately with the kofte.

5

WHAT TO DRINK

Coriander is a difficult flavour to match with wine, but a dry country red from Greece would fit the bill.

Marinated Lamb & Vegetable Kebabs

ACCOMPANY THESE DELICIOUS KEBABS, MARINATED IN SPICY YOGURT, WITH A RICE AND PEPPER PILAF, OR SERVE THEM GREEK-STYLE INSIDE HOT PITTA BREAD

SERVES 4

20 MINS TO PREPARE, PLUS MARINATING

25 MINS TO COOK

280 KCAL PER SERVING

14 green cardamom pods
1 tbls cumin seeds
6 tbls Greek yogurt
2 garlic cloves, crushed
450g / 1lb lamb neck fillets
450g / 1lb courgettes
2 tbls olive oil
2 tsp fresh thyme or 1 tsp dried
1 tsp lemon juice
lemon wedges, to serve

1 Lightly crush the cardamom pods with the flat side of a knife blade to open them. Place in a mortar with the cumin and crush with a pestle.

2 Put the yogurt into a large bowl and add the spices and the garlic. Cut the lamb into 25mm/1in cubes and stir into the yogurt mixture. Cover and marinate in the fridge for at least 6 hours, preferably overnight, stirring once.

3 Cut the courgettes into 25mm/1in slices and mix with the oil, thyme and lemon juice. Leave to marinate for 30 minutes.

4 Heat the grill to medium. Remove the lamb from the marinade, discarding any cardamom pods that stick to the meat. Thread alternating pieces of lamb and courgette on to eight skewers. Grill for 20 - 25 minutes or until the meat has browned and the courgette slices have softened. Serve hot, with lemon wedges.

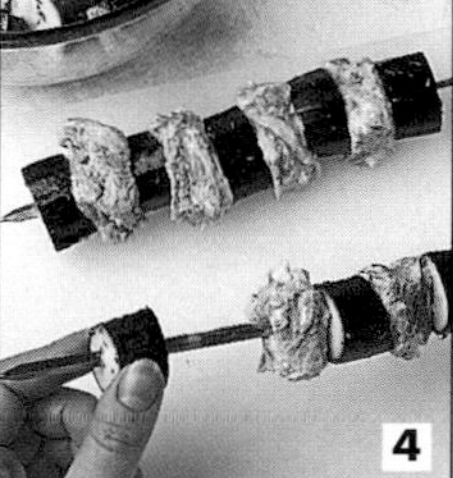

WHAT TO DRINK

A rosé from Provence would be ideal to drink with this spicy lamb dish.

NUTRITION NOTES

The lamb we've used in this recipe is less fatty than other cuts but is still high in protein, iron and B vitamins.

COOK'S TIPS

If you don't have a pestle and mortar simply crush the cardamom and cumin seeds on a chopping board with the end of a rolling pin or a meat hammer. But put them in a plastic bag first, so they don't spill all over the floor.

Middle Eastern Lamb Casserole

It's the exotic spices and dried fruit that conjure up the taste of the Middle East in this distinctive, yet simple, lamb casserole

SERVES 4

25 MINS TO PREPARE

1½ HRS TO COOK

555 KCAL PER SERVING

100g / 4oz 'no-soak' dried apricots
4 tbls olive oil
900g / 2lb boneless shoulder of lamb, cut into 5cm / 2in chunks
1 large onion, thinly sliced
25mm / 1in cube fresh root ginger, peeled and finely chopped
salt and pepper
1 cinnamon stick
2 cloves
finely grated zest of 1 large lemon
50g / 2oz dried cherries
finely chopped fresh mint or parsley, to garnish (optional)

3

4

1 Blend the apricots with 150ml/5fl oz water in a food processor or blender until puréed.

2 Heat the oil in a flameproof casserole over medium heat. Add the lamb, in batches if necessary, and cook until browned. Remove the lamb with a slotted spoon and set aside.

3 Put the onion and ginger in the casserole and cook for 3 - 5 minutes, stirring frequently, until the onions are tender. There shouldn't be much more than 1 tbls of oil in the pan – if there is, spoon off the excess. Return the lamb to the casserole. Pour over 575ml/1pt water and bring to the boil. Use a slotted spoon to remove any grey-brown film that rises to the surface.

4 Stir in salt to taste, cinnamon, cloves and lemon zest. Cover and cook over a very low heat for 45 minutes, stirring occasionally. Stir in the puréed apricots and the cherries and cook for a further 20 minutes or until the cherries are soft and plump.

5 Remove the cinnamon and cloves, sprinkle with fresh herbs (if using) and serve.

INGREDIENTS GUIDE

Dried cherries are available in many large supermarkets and specialist shops. If you cannot find them in a store near you, you can replace them with dried raisins or sultanas – they will provide the same sweetness and have a similar texture.

Lamb & Vegetable Couscous

IN THIS MOROCCAN CLASSIC, TENDER LAMB AND VEGETABLES ARE SERVED ATOP A MOUND OF COUSCOUS. DINERS CAN ADD A DAB OF THE HOT SAUCE CALLED HARISSA IF THEY WISH

SERVES 6

30 MINS TO PREPARE, PLUS SOAKING

1¾ HRS TO COOK

420 KCAL PER SERVING

450g / 1lb lamb, cut in 4cm / 1½in cubes
2 onions, chopped
5 tbls olive oil
½ tsp turmeric
1 tsp ground ginger
2 tbls chopped parsley
2 tsp salt
1½ tsp freshly ground black pepper
575ml / 1pt beef stock
450g / 1lb couscous
4 carrots, quartered
2 small turnips, quartered
4 small courgettes, quartered
400g / 14oz tinned chickpeas, drained
50g / 2oz pine nuts
100g / 4oz raisins, soaked in hot water and drained
harissa, to serve

1

3

1 For this recipe you need a large, deep saucepan in which a colander fits snugly; the bottom of the colander should not touch the stew. Put the lamb, onions, 4 tbls oil, the spices, parsley, salt and pepper in the pan and cook over medium heat, stirring occasionally, for 10 minutes. Add the stock and bring to the boil; lower the heat and simmer for 1 hour.

2 Meanwhile, put the couscous in a bowl and stir in 575ml/1pt cold water. Immediately drain in a sieve and return to the bowl. Allow to stand for 10 - 15 minutes; as the grains swell, break up any lumps with your fingers. Turn into the colander which you have lined with muslin.

3 After cooking for 1 hour, add the carrots and turnips to the lamb and put the uncovered colander with the couscous over the pan. If any steam escapes from the join between the pan and colander, wrap a strip of foil around the top of the pan and fold over the edge of the colander to seal. Cook for 20 minutes. Lift off the colander and add the courgettes and chickpeas. Replace the colander and cook for a further 10 - 15 minutes or until the meat and couscous are tender.

4 Meanwhile, heat the remaining oil in a frying pan over low heat and fry the pine nuts for 3 - 5 minutes or until lightly browned. Stir in the raisins and cook for 1 minute.

5 To serve, spoon the couscous onto a large plate and, using a slotted spoon, pile on the lamb and vegetables. Pour half the cooking broth over the couscous and garnish with the pine nuts and raisins. Serve with the remaining broth in a bowl, accompanied by the harissa.

COOK'S TIPS

This is the traditional way to cook couscous, but there is a quicker method. Shortly before serving, put the grain and a little salt in a bowl and pour over 700ml/1¼pt boiling water. Stir with a fork, cover and leave to stand for 5 minutes. Fluff up with a fork and serve.

Rice Pilaf with Currants

PILAF IS RICE COOKED IN A STOCK UNTIL ALL THE LIQUID HAS BEEN ABSORBED AND THE RICE IS TENDER. HERBS, SPICES AND OTHER FLAVOURINGS MAY ALSO BE ADDED

SERVES 4

10 MINS TO PREPARE

40 MINS TO COOK

375 KCAL PER SERVING

25g / 1oz pine nuts
50g / 2oz butter
1 small onion, chopped
225g / ½lb basmati rice
½ tsp ground coriander
½ tsp salt
575ml / 1pt chicken stock
25g / 1oz currants
fresh coriander, to garnish

1 Dry fry (add no oil) the pine nuts in a heavy pan until lightly golden, or toast them under a medium grill.

2 Melt the butter in a saucepan. Add the onion and cook over low heat for 5 minutes or until softened, stirring frequently.

3 Wash the rice under cold running water. Drain thoroughly. Add to the onions and cook for 1 minute, stirring constantly.

4 Stir in the ground coriander, salt and chicken stock, then cover and simmer for 20 minutes until the liquid has been absorbed.

5 Remove the pan from the heat and stir in the pine nuts and currants. Adjust the seasoning to taste. Cover and leave to stand for 5 minutes. Fork or 'fluff' the rice just before serving. Garnish with fresh coriander.

SERVING SUGGESTIONS

This dish makes a delicious accompaniment to spicy casseroles, curries or even simpler dishes, like roast chicken.

VARIATIONS

You could make this rice pilaf with 1 tbls freshly chopped coriander and 1 tbls sesame seeds in place of the ground coriander and pine nuts. For vegetarians, make the pilaf with vegetable stock.

3

4

5

WHAT TO DRINK

Pick a fruity red wine such as a Beaujolais to balance the spicy flavour of coriander.

Fruit & Almond Filo Pastries

THESE LITTLE PASTRY FINGERS ARE RICH AND SWEET, AND ONE OR TWO WILL FINISH A MIDDLE EASTERN MEAL OFF DELIGHTFULLY

MAKES 15 PASTRIES

30 MINS TO PREPARE

50 MINS TO COOK

215 KCAL PER SERVING

SUITABLE FOR VEGETARIANS

for the filling:
450g / 1lb mixed dried figs, apricots and dates, very finely chopped
100g / 4oz blanched almonds, chopped
100g / 4oz apricot jam
1 tsp ground cinnamon

for the syrup:
150g / 5oz sugar
3 tbls clear honey
1 tbls rosewater

for the pastries:
450g / 1lb filo pastry
100g / 4oz melted butter, plus extra for greasing

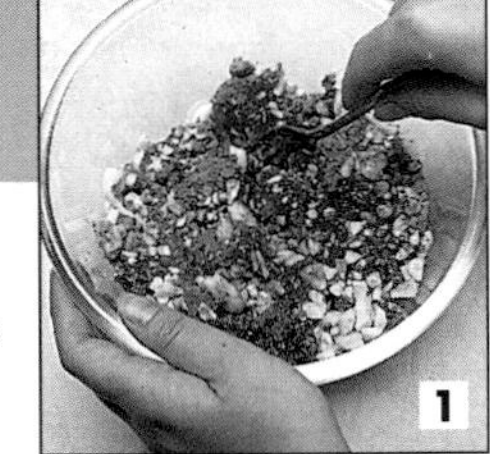

1 To make the filling, combine the dried fruit, almonds, jam and cinnamon in a mixing bowl and blend together well with a fork. Alternatively, place in a food processor or blender and work for just a few seconds. Set aside.

2 Dissolve the sugar in 100ml/3½fl oz water in a heavy pan over medium heat and bring to the boil. Reduce the heat and simmer for 10 minutes. Remove from the heat and stir in the honey and rosewater. Set aside to cool.

3 Heat the oven to 180°C/350°F/gas 4. Work with one sheet of filo pastry at a time, keeping the rest between two pieces of clingfilm, covered by a damp tea towel. Cut two pieces of filo measuring 25x15cm/10x6in. Brush one piece with melted butter and lay the other on top; brush this with melted butter.

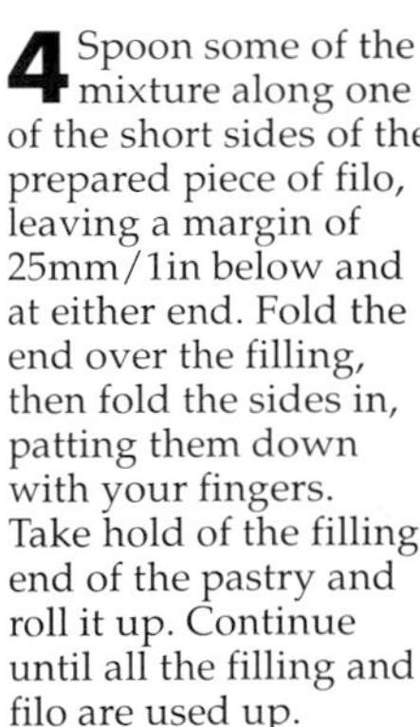

4 Spoon some of the mixture along one of the short sides of the prepared piece of filo, leaving a margin of 25mm/1in below and at either end. Fold the end over the filling, then fold the sides in, patting them down with your fingers. Take hold of the filling end of the pastry and roll it up. Continue until all the filling and filo are used up.

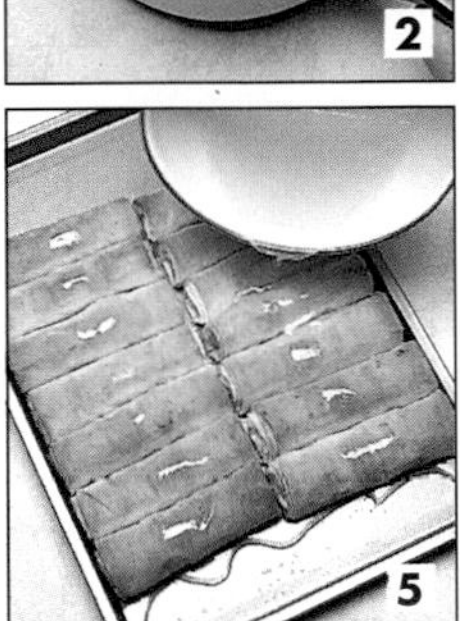

5 Grease a baking sheet with the extra butter and place the pastries, seam side down, on it. Bake for 35 minutes. Remove from the oven and push the pastries together until they are just touching. Pour on the syrup and set aside to cool. Any unused pastries will keep for a few days in an airtight tin in a cool place.

Pumpkin in Syrup

THIS SWEET DESSERT, DELICATELY FLAVOURED WITH ROSEWATER, MAKES AN EXCELLENT END TO ANY MEAL AND IS PARTICULARLY REFRESHING AFTER A SPICY MIDDLE EASTERN FEAST

SERVES
4 - 6

5 MINS
TO PREPARE

1 HR 10 MINS
TO COOK

311 KCAL
PER
SERVING

SUITABLE
FOR
VEGETARIANS

1.4kg / 3lb pumpkin, peeled and de-seeded
175g / 6oz granulated sugar
6 tbls water
2 tsp rosewater
75g / 3oz shelled pistachio nuts, chopped

1 Cut the pumpkin into chunky strips approximately 10x1.5cm/4x½in. Layer the pumpkin strips with the sugar in a large, heavy-based saucepan.

2 Pour over the water and cover the pan tightly. Place the pan over very low heat and cook slowly for about 50 minutes or until the pumpkin is tender, checking occasionally to see that the pan is not boiling dry and adding more water if necessary.

3 Remove the pumpkin slices from the pan, increase the heat and boil rapidly to reduce the liquid to a syrup. Stir in the rosewater, then pour the syrup into a serving dish and leave to cool.

4 Arrange the pumpkin slices on serving plates, pour over the syrup and scatter over the pistachio nuts.

1

2

3

WHAT TO DRINK

Monbazillac from Southern France will probably suit this sweet, nutty dessert very well.

INGREDIENTS GUIDE

Rosewater is sold in most delicatessens and good supermarkets, and you can even buy triple-strength rosewater at the chemist for cooking purposes. Many Middle Eastern desserts and sweets use rosewater in their sweet dishes, but be careful not to add too much when using it at home, otherwise the flavour may become overpowering.

Index

All pictures MC Picture Library